PSYCHOLOGICAL MANIPULATION

The Best Guide to Learn How to Detect and Survive Manipulation When Others Use It to Control Your Life

By

Jake Bishops

Table of Contents

Introduction 9
Manipulative People Common Traits 9

Chapter 1. Manipulation 11
The Mental Health Effects of Manipulation 13

Manipulation When It Shows Up in Relationships 16

Examples of Manipulative Behavior 16

Chapter 2. The Logic behind Psychological Manipulation
.... 19
Gaslighting 21

Projection 26

Chapter 3. What Is Dark Psychology and by Whom Is Used 28

Chapter 4. The Psychology of Body Language 36
Cultural Differences 37

Study Other People's Movements 37

  Eye Contact 39

  Mouth Movements 40

  Nodding 41

  Hands and Arms 42

Chapter 5. Brainwashing 44

The Cultish Brain 46

Brainwash, Abuse, and Stockholm Syndrome 47

   A Recipe for Brainwashing *48*

   Depersonalization *49*

   Acclimation *49*

   Conditioning *50*

   Hypnosis *51*

Chapter 6. Seduction of Dark Psychology 53

Why Use Dark Seduction? 54

Dark Seduction Techniques 55

   The Friendly Opener *56*

   Show Off (A Little Bit) *56*

   Be Mean (But Again, Just a Little Bit) *57*

   Send Mixed Signals *57*

   Give the Ego a Nice, Long Stroke *58*

   Be a Little Bit Taboo *58*

Chapter 7. The Dark Core of Personality 62

A Major Fact Box of Dark Psychology 70

Chapter 8. When the Opponent Is a Manipulator 72

Golden Key 72

Become a Mythical Person 73

Arouse Emotions 73

The State of the Interlocutor 74

Pain Points, Weaknesses, Fears, Doubts 75

Play on Weaknesses *75*

We Are Not Robots; Robots Are Not We 77

Territory Development 77

The Best Alternative to Negotiations 78

Let the Walls Help You 78

Who Is Around? *80*

Leeway *80*

Where Is the World Heading? *81*

Chapter 9. Setting Boundary Not to Be Manipulated... 82

Misconception #1: I May Look Self-Centered If I Set Boundaries 82

Misconception #2: Boundaries Are Symptoms of Disobedience and Un-Submissiveness 83

Misconception # 3: Setting Limits Indicates I Am Always Upset 84

Misconception #4: When I Begin Creating Borders, I Might Be Injured by Others 85

Misconception #5: When I Set Limits I Might Injure Others .. 86

Misconception #6: Boundaries Might Become Difficult to Accept 87

Misconception #7: Boundaries May Result in Feelings of Guilt 89

Conclusion 91

How to Avoid Being Manipulated 91

© Copyright 2021 by Jake Bishops - All rights reserved.

This Book is provided with the sole purpose of providing relevant information on a specific topic for which every reasonable effort has been made to ensure that it is both accurate and reasonable. Nevertheless, by purchasing this Book, you consent to the fact that the author, as well as the publisher, are in no way experts on the topics contained herein, regardless of any claims as such that may be made within. As such, any suggestions or recommendations that are made within are done so purely for entertainment value. It is recommended that you always consult a professional before undertaking any of the advice or techniques discussed within.

This is a legally binding declaration that is considered both valid and fair by both the Committee of Publishers Association and the American Bar Association and should be considered as legally binding within the United States.

The reproduction, transmission, and duplication of any of the content found herein, including any specific or extended information, will be done as an illegal act regardless of the end form the information ultimately takes. This includes copied versions of the work, physical, digital, and audio unless express consent of the Publisher is provided beforehand. Any additional rights reserved.

Furthermore, the information that can be found within the pages described forthwith shall be considered both accurate and truthful when it comes to the recounting of facts. As such, any use, correct or incorrect, of the provided information will render the Publisher free of responsibility as to the actions taken outside of their direct purview. Regardless, there are zero scenarios where the original author or the Publisher can be deemed liable in any fashion for any damages or hardships that may result from any of the information discussed herein.

Additionally, the information in the following pages is intended only for informational purposes and should thus be thought of as universal. As befitting its nature, it is presented without assurance regarding its prolonged validity or interim quality. Trademarks that are mentioned are done without written consent and can in no way be considered an endorsement from the trademark holder.

Introduction

Psychological manipulation involves actions of mental distortion and emotional exploitation to exert control over a person, to obtain a certain benefit or objective. Unlike healthy social influence, a common phenomenon in constructive win-win relationships, the emotional manipulator takes advantage of his victim by generating an imbalance of power that he uses to his advantage. When this type of relationship is established, there is a clear "winner": the emotional manipulator, and a "loser": his victim.

Manipulative People Common Traits

1. **Egocentrism.** Manipulative people do not usually think about what their victim needs, feels, or wants. Because of their egocentric perspective of the world, they continually put their own interests and needs before those of others.
2. **Lack of empathy.** The high level of egocentrism of manipulative people prevents them from putting themselves in the place of others. They have little empathy for the problems and needs of those around them. In extreme cases, they do not even see others as people but as means to achieve their goals.
3. **Irresponsibility.** Manipulative people tend to run away from responsibilities, they do not assume the consequences

of their actions because they do not believe that taking advantage of other people's weaknesses is a bad thing. Even if they hurt others, they will not feel remorse.

4. **Machiavellianism.** Manipulative people tend to score high on the Machiavellianism trait, which means they are adept at creating scenarios and dynamics that foster intrigue, rivalry, and jealousy.

5. **Ease in detecting others' weaknesses.** These people are very skilled at detecting the weaknesses of others, to use them to their advantage. They take advantage of emotional sensitivity and, above all, kindness, because they know that it is easier to manipulate people who are sensitive and willing to help.

Chapter 1.
Manipulation

Manipulation is a topic that most people are going to turn their noses up at. They do not like the idea that comes with it, and they assume that they are above and beyond using these kinds of techniques. Each of us uses manipulation in some form or another to get what we want, even though most of us are not going to do it at the expense of someone else in the process.

To help us out with this, we need first to take a look at manipulation and what it is all about. Manipulation is going to be the practice of using some indirect tactics to control the relationships, emotions, decisions, and even behavior over the target and how they react to things. This is often going to use a lot of different options that you are allowed to use including persuasion, mind control, deception, and more to get what they want.

Most people are going to use some form of manipulation at some point or another in their lives. For example, if you have ever had a day that wasn't going well or you weren't feeling that good, but you told someone who asked that you were doing "fine" then this is a form of manipulation. This is considered manipulation because it is going to control the perceptions and the reactions that the other person has concerning you. Even if you did it to avoid a confrontation, to avoid having someone pity you, or some other reason, it still changed these perceptions of you.

Manipulation, at least the way that we often think about it, and the manipulation that is used in dark psychology, is going to have consequences that are often more insidious. This can sometimes include some form of emotional abuse, especially if the manipulator is in an intimate relationship with the other person. This is why a lot of us assume that all forms of manipulation are bad, but we will hold this opinion, even more, when we see that it harms the mental health, emotional health, and physical health of the other person who is the target.

While people who are the manipulators are going to do this to their target because they want to have some control over their surroundings and environment, the urge to do the manipulation is indeed going to stem from some anxiety and fear that is deep down. In any case, it is not going to be seen as a behavior that is all that healthy for either party.

Engaging in manipulation is going to seem like a great idea to the one who is manipulating. It allows them to gain the control that they want, and they get to receive whatever they wanted in the process. However, when they use this tactic, it is not only going to cause some harm to the other person, the target, it is going to make it hard for the manipulator to connect with their authentic self and get the benefits that come with that.

The Mental Health Effects of Manipulation

If manipulation is not addressed in the manner that it should be, there are going to be a lot of mental health concerns that the target is going to have to deal with. While we all may be manipulated at one point or another, most of the time it is seen as harmless and we don't need to worry about it. But when the target is manipulated on a chronic and consistent basis in close relationship to the manipulator, it could be a sign that some kind of emotional abuse is going on at the same time. Depending on the individual, this is going to show up similar to a form of trauma as well.

There are a lot of different signs and symptoms that can show up when someone has been manipulated for a longer period. Some of the signs of a victim of chronic manipulation can include:

- They will always put the needs of someone else before their own, no matter how bad it may hurt them or how much the other person is asking of them.
- They are used to lying and covering up for the feelings that they have.

- They are always working to make the person who is manipulative as happy as possible, but it always seems like they are failing.
- Their coping patterns are not as healthy as they should be.
- Many targets of manipulation are going to develop deep anxiety.
- Those who are the targets of manipulation are often going to have some level of depression to work through as well.
- Those who have gone through this kind of manipulation for a longer period may find that it is really difficult for them to put their trust in anyone else.

There are some cases when the manipulation is going to become so pervasive that it will cause a victim to start questioning the perception that they have when it comes to reality. A good example of this is the movie "Gaslight." This story shows us how her husband subtly manipulated one woman for a long time. This was so persistent that the wife started to no longer trust what she saw or her perceptions of things. For example, the husband was able to turn down the gaslights and then convinced his wife that the dimming light she was seeing was just something in her head, not a part of reality.

While most of us are not immune to using manipulation at some point or another, a chronic pattern of manipulation can indicate that there could be a sign that there is a health concern mentally to work with.

Studies have shown that manipulation is going to be common when it comes to personality disorder diagnoses, including narcissistic personality and borderline personality. For many people who are dealing with BPD, manipulation is going to be the means that the patient can meet some of their needs emotionally or that they can obtain the validation that they need. And the manipulation in these cases is more often to occur when the person with BPD feels like they are abandoned or insecure. This doesn't excuse the behavior or makes it any better, but it does explain the kind of person who is most likely to use this kind of technique.

Now there are also going to be patients who are dealing with narcissistic personality disorder going to have many different reasons why they will want to use manipulation. When we encounter someone who has NPD, it is easy to see that they run into issues forming close relationships, they may end up turning themselves into the victim to help make sure that their partner is going to stay in the relationship. They are also likely to use a few of the other techniques that come with manipulation, including gaslighting, controlling, playing the victim, blaming, and shaming.

Manipulation When It Shows Up in Relationships

When it comes to manipulation that stays around for the long term, we will quickly find that it can have a big effect on the relationships that we have. This can include the relationship that we have between our romantic partners, family members, and even friends. When it is used for too long and too often, manipulation is going to run the health of any kind of relationship. And for the target, it is going to result in poor mental health. Over time, the target is going to catch on to what is happening or get sick of the way that the relationship makes them feel, and they will leave.

Let's look at how manipulation is used in a marriage or another partnership. Manipulation is going to cause one of the partners; this one is the target to feel like they are worthless, isolated, and bullied. Parents who decide to manipulate their children and this can set the child up for a lot of problems in the future as well. This has been shown to result in many mental health conditions, eating issues, anxiety, depression, and guilt in these children.

Examples of Manipulative Behavior

There are a wide variety of behaviors that can be considered manipulative, especially when they end up causing some kind of harm to the other person in the process. Sometimes, someone can manipulate another one without really realizing what they are doing. But then some are going to do this kind of manipulation to help them get better at it in the future or to help them get what they want out of life. Some of the signs that we can see when it comes to manipulative behavior will include:

- They will isolate the target from loved ones and friends to help change up the perception of that target.
- They will keep out some of the most important information that they have in the hopes of convincing the target to act in a certain way.
- They are dishonest and lie from the very beginning.
- They will imply a threat to keep the target where they are.
- There will be a lot of passive-aggressive behavior from the manipulator towards their target.
- Use of sex to help the manipulator to achieve their own goals.
- Verbal abuse.

As the motives behind this kind of manipulation are going to vary and can be something that is done without much thinking, or it can be done with the intent to harm the target to give the manipulator what they want. But no matter what method is going on here, it is so important for the target and others to identify the circumstances that come with manipulation and how they can deal with it. While breaking things off with the manipulator as soon as possible may be so critical when it comes to situations of abuse, a therapist can help others learn how to deal with or confront the manipulative kind of behavior that they are getting from others.

While we are focusing more on the dark psychology that comes with manipulation, you will find that there are examples of using manipulation that can occur in our daily lives. Often we don't think that we are doing it at all. We think of manipulation as the way that we can get what we want from other people, but sometimes we do it to save the feelings of the other person. For example, how many times have you lied to someone to let them know they looked good in something, even though you didn't think so. You did this to spare their feelings, whether they are a family member or a close friend!

Even though the point of doing this was good, you still were looking to save yourself. You didn't want to be the one who said something means about the other person and how they looked this kind of manipulation may be seen as a good thing though because it was done to spare the feelings of the other person in the process.

Chapter 2.
The Logic behind Psychological Manipulation

Psychological manipulation is defined as a form of social influence that seeks to alter the behavior and the perceptions of others, by the use of tactics that are indirect, deceptive, and underhanded. In other words, it's about using certain tricks to get people to act in a certain way or to think certain things, usually to the advantage of whoever is perpetrating the manipulation.

This way, the interests of the manipulator are advanced, usually at the expense of the other person in that equation. Psychological manipulation employs methods that are both devious and exploitative, and they are often used by people who have one or more of the dark personality traits.

Now, from the very start, we need to make sure you understand that not all psychological manipulation and social influence is negative. It's possible to manipulate someone for their own good. For instance, parents may manipulate their children into eating vegetables. In as much as that is manipulation, it ends up benefiting the child because his or her health is improved. Similarly, friends, family members, and healthcare professionals may try to influence you using certain manipulation techniques with the aim of getting you to make the right choices in certain situations.

Social influence is a normal and important part of social discourse. In healthy social influence, there is no aspect of coercion. In other words, when a well-meaning person tries to influence you, and you resist that influence, they are not going to strong-arm you into doing what they want. However, in unhealthy psychological manipulation, the manipulator often resorts to coercive techniques if they sense that you are resistant to the softer techniques that they have been trying to use on you.

When malicious people deploy psychological manipulation techniques against you, they usually try to conceal the aggressive nature of their intentions, so you have to understand that most of their techniques are designed to be subtle. Most of them will also take some time to get to know you and understand your psychological vulnerabilities before they can decide which manipulation techniques will work on you. This means that just because you have known someone for a while, and you haven't seen them try to harm you in any way, it doesn't guarantee the fact that their intentions are pure, which means that you shouldn't start disregarding your instincts about them. The best manipulators are those who reveal their intentions long after you have decided to trust them.

Remember that manipulators generally tend to ruthlessness, so even if they are treating you well at the beginning of your association with them, pay close attention to the way they act towards others. If you see them using manipulation techniques against other people, you should know that it's just a matter of time before they get around to using the same techniques against you.

We discuss the most common psychological manipulation techniques that are used by people who mean to harm you or to take advantage of you. It's important to understand these techniques and how they work so that you can be able to spot them when they are being used against you or someone close to you, and so that you can know how to defend against them.

Gaslighting

Gaslighting is one of the most lethal psychological manipulation techniques out there. It's where a manipulator tries to get their target to start questioning their own reality. It involves getting someone to doubt their own memories and perceptions, and instead, to start believing what the manipulator wants them to believe.

The manipulator will sow seeds of doubt in the person so that they start thinking that either they remember things wrong, or they are losing their sanity. Gaslighting involves the persistent denial of things that obvious facts. It also involves a lot of misdirection, contradictions, and blatant lying. When a person is subjected to gaslighting for a long time, they start to become unstable, and they start feeling as though their own beliefs are illegitimate.

One common example of gaslighting is where an abuser convinces the victim that the abusive incident she recalls did not even occur. This phenomenon is more common than you might imagine, and it happens in all sorts of relationships. An abusive spouse might deny ever abusing you when confronted later, by either blatantly denying that the abuse occurred, or claiming that it didn't happen as you remember and that your version of the events is greatly exaggerated.

A manipulative boss or colleague might prey on a subordinate and later deny that it happened that way. Someone who groped you might later claim that they "accidentally brushed against you," and they may insist on it so much, to the point that you start thinking that maybe you were mistaken.

You may wonder; "How does it even work? I mean, I have a firm grasp of my own reality, and I doubt someone could be able to convince me that my perceptions are wrong!"

It's easy to assume that gaslighting won't work on you because you are smart or because you are strong-willed, but the truth is that when a manipulator is good at what he is doing, you might not even see it coming. The way it works is that it often starts with small lies on the manipulator's part and small concessions on your part.

Say, for example, your boyfriend shows up a few minutes late to an appointment when you had agreed to meet at a specific time, and he insists that he is on time and that it's you who came in a bit earlier and is mistaken about the timing that you agreed upon. At that moment, you might think, "Well, a 10-minute difference isn't such a big deal, and maybe we just got our lines crossed." You could dismiss this small discrepancy because it seems inconsequently, but that will just be the beginning. The next time, the lie will get a little bigger, and you will feel obligated to excuse it as well, because you already let something else slide, so it would seem inconsistent if you made a big fuss at this point.

After that initial seed is sown, the lies will start to escalate, and you will continue making concessions and agreeing with things that you know are lies, until one day, you realize that you are so far gone. You might not even notice when the small lies graduate into bigger lies. In every step of the way, you will be letting go of your reality and accepting the other person's version of things, and you will find yourself trusting their judgment over your own.

In a nutshell, gaslighting involves desensitizing you to your own reality, until the truth becomes what the other person says it is.

Gaslighting is more likely to work in situations where there is a power dynamic between two people, or between a person and a group of people. In a relationship where the victim is financially or emotionally dependent on the manipulator, the victim may accept to let go of her reality because it's more comfortable to do so than to stand up to the manipulator, only to end up losing the relationship. In the workplace, a subordinate may go along with the boss's lies because he is afraid of losing his job. In a situation where a leader gaslight his followers, it often works because deep within, the followers want to believe whatever lies the leader is telling them.

There are several techniques that gaslighters use to get a stranglehold on their victims. One such technique is withholding. This is where the manipulator refuses to listen to what the victim says or pretends not to understand what they are saying. You might bring up something important, but the response you get is, "I don't even remember this thing you keep talking about."

Another gaslighting technique is called countering. This is where the manipulator questions the victim's memory of the events in question. They say things like "Were you even sober? Because that is not how that happened." The manipulator would then go on to offer an entirely different version of the story where he casts himself as the hero or even the "real victim."

Gaslighters also use blocking and diverting as a manipulation technique. This is where they change the story or question the way the victim is thinking to avoid addressing whatever issue the victim is raising.

Trivializing is also a common gaslighting technique. This is where the manipulator makes the victim feel that her feelings or needs aren't that important, or that she is just being unnecessarily dramatic. Manipulators in such cases may say things like "don't blow things out of proportion."

You may be able to tell if someone is gaslighting you if you find that you are frequently second-guessing yourself, or that your convictions fade away when you interact with a certain person. If a person makes you ruminate about certain character flaws, they are most likely gaslighting you. Someone who tells you that you are too emotional might really be trying to get you to stop trusting your emotions. If you feel confused about the nature of your relationship, or you feel like the person is driving you crazy, or that you are losing control when you are with them, they might be gaslighting you.

If you walk into a room to discuss something specific, but a few moments later, you find yourself arguing with your partner about a whole other topic, it means that the person is deliberately frustrating your genuine efforts to communicate, and it could be a sign of gaslighting.

If you feel fuzzy about your own beliefs, thoughts, and feelings whenever you are with someone, that is a clear red flag. When you are being gaslighted, you might also find that you are constantly apologizing for "being mistaken" or that you are frequently making excuses to yourself and others for your partner's behavior.

Projection

Projection is a psychological manipulation technique where someone transfers their emotions and mistakes onto you. Projection is a defense mechanism that almost everyone uses to some extent. We all have a natural tendency to project our negative emotions and undesirable feelings onto the people around us, and this often happens when we feel like we have been put on the spot. However, in as much as we all do it, narcissists and people with other dark personality traits tend to do it excessively and to absurd extents.

Toxic people find it very difficult to admit even to them that the nasty things around them could be a result of their own doing, and they always find people to blame for every little thing that happens. Such people often go out of their way to avoid taking responsibility for their own actions. As a result, they may assign their negative behavior and traits to you. For example, if you have a boss who is always late to work, you might be surprised to find him accusing you of tardiness, even if you are consistently punctual. A kleptomaniac is more likely to accuse you of stealing his/her personal items.

Chapter 3.
What Is Dark Psychology and by Whom Is Used

In general terms, psychology involves understanding and studying human behavior with a major concentration on how they think, how they act, and how they interact. This is the aspect that deals with the study of the human mind. The science of manipulation and mind control is referred to as dark psychology. No one would love to fall victim to manipulation, but this happens most of the time.

Most people that use dark psychology are people who have an inflated sense of their worth as individuals, and they always need other people to help put validation into what they believe about them being superior. In doing this, they use manipulation and unethical persuasion. Another set of people are those who are emotionally unable to handle the fact of them being impulsive. In the same vein, politicians, salespeople, public speakers, and even leaders use these dark tactics.

However, in dark psychology, we study human issues relating to the psychological nature of them to be able to feed upon other people using instincts and social sciences theory. Dark psychology, being a universal part of the human condition, assumes that any behavior portrayed by someone is purposeful and hereby is motivated to achieve a goal. For example, everybody always has their mind focused on who a criminal is because they are seen as people that should be rejected in society because of their flawed background and maybe upbringing. But in society today, the number of harms done to the public is usually from a corporate system such as government officials and major CEO. There are crimes that most times are not detected and are hard to bring justice to. Dark psychology explains that the dark behavior of people is often developmental such that it is related to how they are being brought up so anyone that acts wicked will be assumed not to have been brought up in a loving and caring way.

Dark psychology will always explain any form of behavior, whether normal or abnormal in a positive way. The major triad of dark psychology is associated with the three words, which are very important to live adaptively. These include sorry, regret, and remorse. The word 'sorry' is an adjective with different types of meaning defining different kinds of communications interactions and expressions in relationships. Sometimes the term stands as a form of apology or an expression of regret. And sometimes, it is an expression of being remorseful. The feeling of being remorseful and communicating regret is necessary for the survival of all humans generally.

You can simply achieve this. Firstly, expect others to offend you, and whether you are innocent or guilty, always initiate an apology with a look of empathy. You need to plan not to want to offend people in the future and, most importantly, always forgive but never forget because this fosters respect.

While interacting whether, with an individual or a group, you will notice that the person that displays the strongest emotion will be the one that will lead the interaction and influence other people's emotions, the same with the dark psychology of all the other people involved.

Same way, when you are in a two-person interaction, if you are displaying a deep sadness and the other person is just a bit happy and joyful. You will notice that you will have a greater influence on the conversation as you have the probability to draw the other person towards being sad.

We humans can be so irrational and emotional at times. You can learn the latest emotional IQ tools in bulk, and yet when you're emotional or triggered by something you are asked messily. There's usually an element of deception in dark psychology. However, it is important to note that deception is necessary to some extent, depending on the kind of result you want to obtain. Deception is not generally an evil concept even though some people use it in extremely evil things, but most times the intentions behind the use of deception are good. It can be said that the use of deception can bring good things sometimes. The major thing is to understand the approach to it. In deceiving people, don't paint the complete picture in lies.

Most times, persuasion is often used by people you love and trust wholly. This tactic involves making compliments of showing affection to someone to make a request, exaggeration or telling partial true stories, holding back affection and attention thereby denying someone of love, and telling a person to do something to motivate them to do the opposite in which is what you really want.

Dark Psychology involves the use of mind tricks, which is in between deception and persuasion. The psychological mind tricks might sound outrageous, but it works well. They are being used to mislead people to think that what they know to be right is wrong, and what they believe to be wrong is right.

In a simple term, dark psychology allows humans to be willing and deliberate to harm others through their decisions and actions, sometimes this might not be physical. However, some emotions are groomed from a very early stage of an individual's life. For example, a child grows to learn how to cry in such a way that the adults around will make themselves available for their bidding. We can call this crying a manipulative tool for the child to be enabled to control people around. As a child grows up, if such a child is not being cautioned on what he's doing, the so-called innocent childish behavior would now become a dark way of controlling people to do what he/she wants.

Dark psychology is a means of studying how a person thinks and also sees a need to understand the intent behind actions and words. In general, it illuminates the dark side of human nature. In dark psychology, the effect is experienced by both the victim and the perpetrator. The personality traits which are considered dark include narcissism, psychopathy, and Machiavellianism.

In a simple term, an excessive admiration of oneself in an obsessive manner towards appearance is referred to as narcissism. Narcissists usually feel superior. They do not subscribe to the rule of giving and take in a normal relationship. They are good at blaming others whenever there is an issue. A common feature is to be an extremely self-centered individual. Narcissists have an unrestricted appetite for control and power. They control people by making them think that they are looking out for them. They are also very smart such that they get involved in your day-to-day activities in life without being noticed. Above all, they are Keen liars and master is the lie skills.

Psychopathy is a trait that is associated with not being sensitive to other people. A psychopath will almost not have empathy for other people. Psychopaths are usually bold, confident, and fearless. They are risk-takers and extremely charming.

On the other hand, the third personality trait is known as Machiavellianism, the term is used to describe someone who lacks emotions and desire to achieve something at the expense of other people's feelings. This can be done through deceit, manipulation, or going against some moral rules. An individual who scores highly in the Machiavellianism test is usually referred to as a "High Mach" These people are always around us, sometimes in our workplace or as a neighbor. They are hard-working people who are smart and are unapologetic about stepping on other people's toes. These sets of people are opportunists and can detach themselves from situations they are in emotionally. Due to this ability, they are capable of involving themselves in several sexual several encounters. They can stand a chance of being good teammates, but certainly not a good friend.

This knowledge of dark psychology is to protect yourself from those personalities when you come across them. Dark psychology cuts across all human conditions, which are universal in nature. It studies how the condition of humans relates to their thoughts, feelings, and perception. The general assumption here is that every human has the potential to be violent. Learning this concept is of two-folded benefits. First, it helps individuals to accept that they tend to become evil, so the knowledge of this will prevent it from erupting. And secondly, it gives everyone a reason to struggle to survive.

This is a technique used in restructuring people's minds on how to get rid of bad habits, how to become productive, and how to make them effective in general. You can use this technique to connect sense, mind, behavior, and language. The technique is designed in such a way that you tend to control people without them even being aware of what you are doing to them.

Neuro refers to the nervous system, which is made up of the mind and all other senses. Your nervous system function when you interact with your environment or people generally that's why when you listen more to people, you get to understand what is being said, also when you pay more attention to what happens around you, you know and see more things about people around.

However linguistic refers to the language, it doesn't necessarily mean the language you speak may be English or Spanish, but it depends more on your usage of words, the underlying tone of your voice, and even the rate at which you communicate with people.

And programming in NLP refers to the act of forming the habit. NLP teaches you how to make sure that the habit you pick is useful to you as a person in your life, and even in your interaction with others. It has been said that it takes approximately 21 days should leave or break and habits formed and 66 days to form a new one. NLP allows you to choose the reality you want for yourself. Also, it helps you to influence other people's reality without them knowing, and this programming relies on other various techniques in which mirroring is one of them.

As the name suggests, mirroring deals with mimicking the behavior of the person you are interacting with in a very subtle way. It is done subtly because the person must not understand what you are doing or else you will not achieve a good result.

In this technique, you must pay attention to the person's body language, tone and tempo of voice, choice of words, vocabulary, and even pattern of thought. The essence of mirroring is to be in oneness with the person you are communicating with.

This technique has also been employed by people to keep a long-term relationship. Psychology explains that when you like someone, you will subconsciously behave like them by mirroring their actions. When you even mirror your potential partner, he/she will be glad to think that you understand them. And, when people have a feeling that you understand them, they become more open to you.

Chapter 4.
The Psychology of Body Language

One of the clearest ways to examine others is to look at their body language. How a person conducts themselves, walks and even talks will give you many clues about them. Each individual has a lot of differences in their body language, and there is no perfect way to understand what it reveals about that person. There are however many common signs within groups of individuals that can begin to give you a profound understanding of how they function. It is not a simple process, because it begins with becoming conscious of your own body language.

To comprehend and seek to resolve the enigma of body language, you need to be hyper-conscious. We have taken you through the journey of becoming conscious of your feelings and where they might emerge from. It is time to focus on being conscious of your body. To understand what makes an individual distinct from others based on their body language, you must first look at yourself and examine how you handle your body. Many people may be more conscious of their actions than they are of their feelings. Women are more inclined to be conscious of their bodies and the space they occupy, mainly because of the male-dominated society in which we grew up. Anyone may find it difficult to scrutinize the way they carry their body. You may lose focus when trying to maintain hyper-consciousness, becoming too insecure with your own body and gestures. Once you get to know someone else's body language better, you can also recognize what makes them special.

Cultural Differences

There are many reasons a person's body language varies, so it is essential to note that not everything about a body expression is 100% accurate for every individual. This is particularly important to keep in mind while talking to people of diverse cultural backgrounds. Some societies exercise modesty, therefore contact may be inappropriate. On the other hand, some cultures may be more receptive to communicating their emotions through their bodies. Consequently, the culture is crucial to consider when talking about how an individual might use their body.

Study Other People's Movements

Once you become more conscious of body movements and what they might mean, you may continue to explore them as you communicate with other individuals. Everyone you come into contact with uses their body to reflect various things. Many individuals are fairly shut down, and others may be more accessible. These are some slight variations that you might notice just by watching someone's body language.

While examining other people's and your own body language, it is important to try to behave naturally. It may be possible to become super-aware of your movements, but remember that you don't have to keep your body in a particular way. Not everyone is as mindful of body movements as you may be, so at the end of the day, don't look too much at your movements.

However, once you start learning the body movements of others, you can begin to understand more about them. When meeting some people you know, some things about them might begin to make sense. You might think one of your friends is pretty arrogant in the way they are carrying themselves or interacting. Some friends could demonstrate how nervous they are with themselves, even though you had always thought they were extremely confident.

Reading the body language of a person and having intuition as to why they may be behaving a certain way will help you to fully understand them at their core, which gives you more influence in persuading them. You may want to match your boss's confidence in making an offer for a boost. Maybe you have found that you need to be calmer around some friends who seem to be reserved or anxious. It can be frightening at first to become conscious of your body language, but soon you will be confident with the way you walk.

Always have a mirror around you to start the process of being comfortable with your own body. When you are eating, watching TV, or even lying in bed, put up a mirror so you can see how you are holding yourself. Once you get an outsider's point of view on how you are moving, you will be able to notice how other people are moving as well.

Eye Contact

Keeping eye contact is one of the most important clues to evaluate who someone is. It is necessary to be cautious of your eye contact use, as it provides other hints about your temperament and true nature. Nevertheless, it is important to keep eye contact to let a person know you are listening to what they are talking about and that they have your maximum attention.

However, it can also be misconstrued and make people think you are trying hard to convince them you are paying attention when you are actually distracted. Sometimes too much eye contact will disturb others as well, so if you observe a person becoming uncomfortable because of the extent of eye contact you have with them, switch it up occasionally. Research has shown that dilation of pupils can be a clear indicator of an individual being attentive to what you are saying. You know that you have their undivided attention and that they are genuinely engaged in the interaction. The reverse—shifty eyes—could imply dishonesty. Someone whose gaze is constantly moving could be trying to persuade you that they are listening. They know they need to attempt to maintain eye contact, but they are completely out of touch with what you are saying. Those with shifting eyes may also be pretending to you or trying to trick you in some manner. They may have trouble keeping eye contact with you because they know they are deceptive.

Mouth Movements

What a person does with their mouth is also very important to know their personality. Someone with closed or pursed lips may be trying to focus, or they may even be trying hard to conceal a sour face. You can also examine the smile of an individual. If the corners of their eyes are not wrinkled, they might be faking a smile. Anyone who fakes a smile is not inherently bad; they might just be worrying about something else too distracted to pay keen attention to what you are saying.

Smiles are sometimes responses to unpleasant circumstances, too. When monkeys grin, it is not because they are pleased, but usually because they expose their teeth as a means to taunt those around them. They can open their mouths widely if they become afraid and anxious, revealing that they have teeth they can use to harm. The same is true for pit bulls. They only display their teeth when they feel endangered. This can often also be the case for humans but on a subconscious level. Nervous laughter and grinning may be a way to relieve a person's anxiety. Some people are only genuinely smiling when they have wrinkles in their eye corners.

An individual who continually covers their mouth is also typically anxious. They could bite their lips or their fingers or place a hand over their mouth. Often understanding that a person is anxious or upset can be useful when attempting to influence them. We will explore how and when to use that knowledge to influence others.

Nodding

How an individual turns and tilts their head can be a discreet movement. Some people are not as conscious of when they move their heads most of the time. The movements of the neck and head of the individual you are examining can give you a better glimpse into what they might be thinking on a deeper level. Someone who nods their head very frequently when speaking to you may just be nervous or trying to terminate the conversation as soon as possible. They are trying to set up a tempo so you can speak faster. They want you to know they are listening to you, but you are not talking fast enough. If somebody is doing this to you, start speeding up your words to keep their concentration.

If someone tilts their head to the side, they may have a genuine interest in what you are saying. They are trying to turn an ear towards you, so they can understand you properly, whether or not they are conscious of their motions. They also show that they are listening to you and that they need you to continue talking. It is a way for them to come closer to you in the discussion without any digressions or interruptions being required. If somebody nods too dramatically, they might just be trying to convince you they are concerned about what you say.

They might realize they ought to pay attention, but they may have lost interest or not comprehend what you are saying, so they nod to make you believe they are keeping up with the conversation. If you see someone around you shaking their head unnaturally, it may be worth either diverting the conversation to get their attention back or explaining yourself better as they might just be lost. Mimicking the movement of someone's head can be very effective in convincing people. A slight turn of the head when listening to them can show you understand what they are saying. It can also demonstrate that you are sympathetic to them, particularly if they are talking about something that seems difficult for them.

Hands and Arms

How someone utilizes their hands and arms is another way that body language can be used to gain a deeper knowledge of the individuals you communicate with. Our hands give away so much about us. They are a way to express tales, putting specific focus on different parts. If somebody is telling a story, they use hand movements to hold their listeners' attention. Think of someone involved in a dialogue as one who is directing an orchestra; they are going to lift their hands to keep up the rhythm and intensity for the listeners around them. The hands and arms of somebody can also convey just how outgoing or withdrawn they are; they could be like a gateway through the body. If someone has their arms closely crossed in front of their chest, that person may be somewhat more closed off, not wanting to participate too much in conversation.

However, having their arms crossed does not automatically indicate that someone is uncommunicative. They may also just want to relax their arms, and if they are hanging loosely in front of them, they are possibly only listening to you passively. Someone who has their arms spread wide, perhaps over their head, would generally be very accessible and maybe even seek to exert control over a situation. Someone might try to assert their dominance with their hands on their waist.

Chapter 5.
Brainwashing

A lot has been said about brainwashing, from its applications in the armed forces to its use in science fiction sleeper agents. The truth lies somewhere in between. Brainwashing first entered the public consciousness during the Korean War, where a group of American GI's were captured and then reportedly brainwashed by their captors. Millions looked at their TV sets in horror as American soldiers denounced their own country and refused to be rescued. Many speculated that they had been brainwashed using ancient oriental techniques—but in truth, the men were probably just tortured. When they were later examined after their release, examiners found all the traditional symptoms of PTSD but no lasting evidence that the men were brainwashed. What the men were suffering from was a combination of trauma and conditioned fear. Still, it had all the hallmarks of what we now consider as brainwash.

Following the war, the US government would start a secret research program called MK ULTRA, which would last for about a decade. In 1973 an FOIA request saw the release of hundreds of documents related to the program, each talking about how the government experimented with LSD, hypnosis, and other brainwashing techniques. Experimental subjects ranged from soldiers to drug addicts and prostitutes. MK ULTRA routinely disregarded basic human experimentation rights and was quite the scandal at the time.

Whether any conclusive technique for brainwashing was discovered by the US government is unknown. But we do have reason to believe that brainwashing, in whatever capacity, is certainly possible and has been used since the 20th century at least. The question becomes not if brainwashing is possible, but what does it entail, and how does it relate to the techniques used. What is the difference, if any, between brainwashing and propaganda? Or brainwashing and religious indoctrination? In all these instances, the victim may act in a certain way that fulfills a greater agenda. During the cold war era, for example, there was mass hysteria and inoculation from communism in the United States. Ordinary citizens were made to hate the foreign ideology of communism—a sentiment that exists even today.

Then there are cases like Patty Hearst; a woman kidnapped in 1974 by a terrorist group calling themselves the Symbionese Liberation Army. By the time she was released from her captors, she was a wanted criminal for several crimes. There is a famous CCTV recording of her and other members of the SLA robbing a bank with long guns. What followed was a public debate about whether Patty was a bonafide criminal or an unwilling participant in a crime. There was also talk that she had been brainwashed by the

SLA, similar to how young Arabic men are radicalized by Islamic terrorist groups today.

For whatever reason, we are more likely to accept "radicalization" than we are to say "brainwashing." Both things point to the same general phenomena, which is an extreme form of depersonalization that results in a radical shift in behavior.

The Cultish Brain

Why on earth would hundreds of people willingly drink Kool-Aid laced with cyanide poison? Why would the same people willingly force their children to drink it as well? The answer is probably some combination of brainwashing, deception, and plain old coercion. People who follow cults tend to have a similar psychological profile to each other. It is a deadly mixture of helplessness, gullibility, and trustfulness.

In a way, the cultish brain has already been softened up for indoctrination. Nothing in the cultish brain tells the follower that what they may be doing is wrong. Couple this with the superficial charm of cult leaders and their false goodwill towards others and you have a situation of extreme misdirection. Whenever the cult leader lashes out or punishes someone, it is accepted. Everyone is so deluded in the Utopian vision of their leader that they never realize who the true psychopath is.

The washing of the cultish brain is perhaps the ultimate application of dark psychology techniques. Everything from charisma, manipulation, and deceit are used to trap followers. Should we consider these people as brainwashed? Most certainly so! And they got into that state simply because they fit a certain psychological profile and a malicious attacker decided to take advantage of it.

There really isn't any magic to it. There is no ancient oriental technique needed, even if it existed. Torture and violence go hand in hand with it but are also not required. A psychological profile and the will to power are all that is needed.

Brainwash, Abuse, and Stockholm Syndrome

The dark psychological technique of using operant conditioning (positive and negative reinforcement) is often likened to brainwash. In it, the victim's behavior is tailored through a series of rewards and punishments. Again, there is nothing mystical or science fiction about making a dog salivates with the ringing of a bell (as per Pavlov's experiments). But the end result is something akin to what is popularly described as brainwash.

Now, within this framework, there is the possibility that the victim is "in on it." People who knew Patty Hearst said that the Patty that they knew was kind and warm-hearted. Never did they imagine that she was capable of terrorism. So, when the audiotapes of

Hearst admitting to joining the SLA were aired on TV, her closest friends and family did not doubt that it was some form of brainwash. As with the captured soldiers during the Korean War, Hearst was likely subjected to torture. She would later admit that the SLA sexually abused her and, in her words, "brainwashed" her.

Others have pointed out that the Patty Hearst case may have been caused by Stockholm syndrome—a positive relationship formed between a hostage and their captors. Clearly, Patty Hearst showed all the signs and symptoms of Stockholm syndrome. This included denouncing her own family and aligning her own belief system with that of the SLA. One can only wonder why Patty Hearst acted in such a way. She even donned a different name amid all the confusion. Assuming a different personality is a common denationalization technique.

It could be that Patty Hearst was simply trying to stay alive in a time of duress. Ultimately, it was the nature of the hostage situation that granted her a presidential pardon by Bill Clinton

A Recipe for Brainwashing

A potential formula for brainwashing someone (controlling their behavior) can be sourced by using dark psychological techniques. The first and perhaps most important step is to select a target who already fits the psychological profile, someone who possesses a cultish brain, for example. If the target does not have that attribute, any attempts to brainwash with this recipe will fail. The cultish brain can either be acquired or inherent. Many of the hallmarks of the cultish brain are just defense mechanisms against previous traumas.

Depersonalization

The first step is to breakdown the target's personality little by little. Gaslighting techniques can be used to attack their sense of self and their belief system. Changing the target's name or insisting that they use a nickname often helps. At the same time, the target needs to have a high sense of dependence. Over time, they must be isolated from their closest support groups and family members. Gaslighting and other forms of deception can pit the victim against such support groups. Discord within these groups (whether real or imagined) will push the victim away. They will seek salvation somewhere else, like the arms of an attacker.

Acclimation

A depersonalized victim does not put up a fight. They do not object when given manufactured truths. They are willing to accept any new identity that you form for them. During the acclimation phase, the victim will require more attention from the manipulator. Brainwashing, in this way, is not a simple solution. It requires dedication over some weeks or months.

Acclimation is completed when the target is no longer their former self. In the case of Patty Hearst, this was the period when audiotapes were recorded of her denouncing her family. Acclimation can manifest itself as a rejection of commonly held beliefs like religion and nationalistic doctrines—a denouncing of ideas and the common belief system of the target. If you do not know what these are, then you cannot gauge their level of acclimation.

Conditioning

After the acclimation phase, the victim is in a very vulnerable state. They are rejecting things that they used to hold as sacred. They are slowly reinventing themselves, with the careful guidance of their manipulator. All that follows is conditioning their behavior in whatever way the manipulator chooses.

Positive reinforcement results in more complicit subjects. The victim is rewarded for their actions, either in the form of attention, money, power, sensual gratification, love, or whatever else it is they require. Positive reinforcement creates more trusting relationships between the manipulated and the manipulator. The downside is that positive reinforcement may not always work. The subject is motivated primarily by their needs. Once those needs are reasonably met, they have little motivation to take risks.

Negative reinforcement is more effective but crueler. It can be done with emotional or even physical abuse. Anything that is punishing enough. Negative reinforcement is like placing the subject in between an anvil and a hammer. The source of punishment is usually their manipulator. It is also possible to construct a situation where the punishment comes from outside or internalized source.

Once the three phases are completed, the subject is far gone from their former selves that they won't recognize their own actions. If done correctly, the change should be dramatic, like a middle school kid acclimatizing to high school and from high school to college. At each one of these stages, there is a radical shift in the maturity and belief system of the student.

Hypnosis

It originated out of a belief that all humans and beasts were controlled by a force called "animal magnetism." And just like regular magnetism, animal magnetism could be manipulated using some form of magnetic force. The father of hypnosis, Franz Mesmer, influenced the term "mesmerize." The type of hypnosis he practiced consisted of hand movements across the body that served to make "mesmeric passes."

Though back then it was widely rejected that hypnosis had anything to do with mysterious forces. The most likely conclusion was that the phenomena were caused by the placebo effect and the participants' own imagination. To hypnotize someone, they had to be looking to be hypnotized. It is used in clinical practice to help psychotherapists unlock suppressed memories in their patients through the power of autosuggestion.

Normally, hypnotherapy takes years to study. A skilled hypnotist can induce a trance-like state in their patients that lie somewhere between waking consciousness and REM sleep. Inside of the hypnotic trance patients are susceptible to the power of suggestion, which the hypnotist may bring attention to. By uttering certain words or phrases, they can make the patient think and even do certain things. The connections that the patient makes are largely on a subconscious level.

Chapter 6.
Seduction of Dark Psychology

Seduction is persuading someone to have sex with you or make them more excited to do so. Seduction is often simply part of attraction between two people, as it sets the stage for the sex to come. It may include a woman wearing lingerie to greet her partner after his long day at work, or a man buying his date a fancy dinner and whispering in her ear how beautiful she looks in her dress. Among good-intentioned people, seduction is a normal, specific mode of communication appropriate for indicating desire and hoping the person of interest feels the same way. Ideally, the process of seduction is never dishonest or misleading. The person being seduced knows what their pursuer wants, and they can have a mutually satisfying sexual encounter or start a romantic relationship.

How does seduction fit into dark psychology then? Seduction can be to help the person being seduced, to hurt that person, or to benefit the person doing the seducing. All three of these motives have one thing in common though; all seduction, to some degree or another, requires at least some affection of the desired person's mental state.

Why Use Dark Seduction?

Dark psychology seduction is often an effective seduction technique because it can make the person of desire feel intrigued and excited. In some ways, it is almost a form of persuasion. At its most ethical, persuasion is beneficial to the person being seduced, and the persuader has good intentions. At its worst, the persuader causes harm to their victim and only thinks of possible rewards to them. The same goes for seduction.

A person with good intentions may use dark psychology seduction techniques to get the most out of their love life. They harbor no will to harm others but know how to have fun. When this person decides to marry, it will most likely be a happy marriage, as they have created excitement and joy in their partner.

Someone who seeks to harm through dark psychology may choose to do so because of the thrill they derive from letting someone down so spectacularly. When this harmful person seduces someone, usually a vulnerable person, they feel pleasure in watching the partner's excitement turn into fear and anguish. This person has no regard for the person they have seduced and is often promiscuous, with a long trial of failed relationships and angry exes behind them.

If someone is completely self-serving with their dark seduction, then their results will fall somewhere between those of the good-intentioned seducer and the maniacal seducer. The completely self-serving seducer may cause harm, but mostly out of selfishness and lack of awareness. In general, this person will often be dissatisfied because their intentions lead them to neglect their relationships with those whom they seduce.

Using some dark psychology when trying to seduce someone is not innately good or evil. Instead, it simply a tactic that has proven more successful than others. The only absolute truth about this method is that it is an efficient way to seduce someone that maximizes one's chances of finding someone they find attractive and enjoyable. With that said, dark seducers are more likely to get what they want because they know what they want. Dark seducers usually get the most attractive, most successful partners because they see what they want and go for it. They are not wishy-washy, and they do not settle out of convenience or loneliness.

Dark Seduction Techniques

There are many techniques to dark seduction, but at the core of this method is creating excitement and joy in whoever you wish to seduce. Be sure to entice this person, make them want you. These techniques are all about creating witty banter and showing off how fun and attractive you are in a suave, smooth, swoop.

The Friendly Opener

This technique involves doing anything but asking "what's your sign" or "come here often?". In this technique, an open-ended question is best. Something like, "Hey there, could you help my friend and I? We disagree with who the most overplayed artist on the radio is right now." See what's happening? The seduce asked a friendly question that opened the floodgates for a funny, friendly conversation. The person being seduced does not feel overpowered or intruded upon. Instead, a friendly stranger asked an interesting question.

The strength of this technique is that it simply invites friendly conversation without mentioning any sex. It is impossible to be rejected because this is not even a sexual advance. It is simply a way of meeting a new person and having some fun banter.

This also works because it avoids coming on too strong. The object of your desires is less likely to feel defensive, suspicious, or intruded upon if you present yourself in a friendly, non-aggressive way. You will not seem overtly sexual or creepy, so this person will not feel the need to avoid you or shut down the conversation as soon as it ends.

Show Off (A Little Bit)

This tactic is all about demonstrating, not just bragging about, social capital and success. The first step is to simply look the part—

wear a nice, noticeable watch or jewelry. Dress unlike everyone else, as it is a sign of a confident, independent thinker. Another important way to show off is not to seem too desperate for company; show up to a bar with a group of friends, or flirt with two women at a time who are friends with each other. This demonstrates to both women that you are not only a bit of a challenge but also that you are a friendly, confident person in general.

Be Mean (But Again, Just a Little Bit)

If the person you are trying to seduce is acting a little bit haughty or clearly playing hard to get, pretend you are about to walk away. They will be wowed by this one because they expected you to keep playing along with their little game. Showing that you are not so desperate that you will put up with game playing from them show you are confident and not in need of their attention because you can simply seek attention elsewhere. Once they want your attention back, you have practically won, because now the person you are interested in feels like they are working a little bit extra for your attention, not the other way around.

Send Mixed Signals

It can work in your favor not to seem too interested. Do not pick up their call every now and then. Maybe once whoever you are interested in seems to reciprocate, hold back just a little bit and cut back contact. Why? Seeming just a tad aloof can create a sense of depth about you, leading your target to wonder even more about you or maybe even become fascinated. This is all about creating an air of value for you. Everyone wants what they can't have. Playing just a little bit hard to get can make someone's interest in your pique.

Give the Ego a Nice, Long Stroke

To stroke someone's ego, do not simply flatter them until you turn blue in the face. Instead, agree with them a lot—go along with what they say, get to know them, and come to understand how this person's emotions work. In doing this, you will comply with the person's belief that they are the main character of their own story. Everyone believes this about themselves because it is true; each person, in their own story of their life, is the main character of that story. By playing along with someone else's story of their own life, you satisfy and validate them, making them trust you and enjoy your presence.

Be a Little Bit Taboo

Most people are, at least to some extent, thrill-seeking. This does not mean that we all seek out dangerous situations or abuse hard drugs to feel alive, but rather that we all crave a little bit of excitement, and the taboo inspires this in us.

Another important facet of dark psychology is to know that you miss one hundred percent of the shots you do not take. Why is this important? A little bit of arrogance and psychopathy is useful here. Most people suffer from an overwhelming fear of rejection when they are trying to flirt. They are so afraid, in fact, that they will avoid going after those they find attractive because they fear how much pain they may feel as a result of rejection. The dark seducer knows a secret, which is that there are billions of fish in the sea, and rejection is not all that bad.

Simply put, learn to take rejection—avoiding it simply makes flirting an even more daunting prospect and adds even more anxiety to dating. Instead, flirt enough that you get some practice with rejection. Once you survive it a few times, it will seem way less intimidating. The dark seducer knows rejection is a blessing in disguise because it simply frees up time in the future to pursue other, more interested prospects.

Rejection creates resilience and will let you figure out what your flirting and seduction style may be. Some people go for a more structured approach, by asking questions and knowing the emotions to evoke in a specific order in the object of their desires. Others, however, may like to go for it more organically by asking an open-ended question or "going with the flow"—of course, projecting confidence and ease throughout the interaction.

While you may have already made up your mind about dark seduction, you must ask, "When does dark seduction turn cruel and unethical?" Dark seduction becomes malevolent when it involves dishonesty, deception, and coercion. There are many ways one may wield dark seduction morally dubiously but knowing what this looks like can prevent you from experiencing a great deal of pain.

Of course, not everyone can be lucky in love. Some people were raised in chaotic households and find themselves in dysfunctional relationships as adults because they were not taught as children how healthy relationships function. Others are young, naïve, and impulsive; the prospect of love is so tempting to them that they are willing to ignore obvious red flags about their dates and dive headfirst into sex and relationships.

There is a different type of serial dater, though. This person does not seem naïve and has a string of failed relationships behind them. Many of us know someone like this—an uncle on his fourth wife or a friend who dates men for short periods, all of whom seem similarly deferent and meek, before discarding them and finding the next one. The serial dating dark seducer, unlike a normal person who has simply dated many people, will often take no responsibility for why their past relationships failed. This is the guy who says, "All my exes are crazy," or "I won't break up with her now even though I don't like her. I'll leave her when I line up someone else to date afterwards." Avoid this person. They discard people callously and use dark seduction to either harm others or benefit only themselves.

Chapter 7. The Dark Core of Personality

Dark psychology is human consciousness as well as constructive study regarding the human condition and human personality since it relates to the nature of psychology where people prey on others.

The character is often motivated by the psychopathic and psychopathological criminal drives that usually lack purpose as well as general assumptions of instincts and drive. It is also driven by evolutionary biology as well as social sciences theory.

All humanity can victimize humans as well as other living creatures successfully.

Although many will restrain from this character, some will take action on their impulses.

Dark psychology is also defined as the art of manipulation as well as mind control. Although psychology is known as the study of the human character and it's central to human thought, interactions, as well as actions, the word Dark Psychology is a great phenomenon where people use various tactics in motivating and persuading others to get what they want.

Dark psychology is also an overview of the existing psychological persuasion that humans have over other people. In the current world, dark psychology is a powerful force that's used in several sectors.

Great influencers across the world also utilize it. Those who aren't aware of the risks of this dark force may have it used against them in different scenarios. To be safe from such harmful elements in society, you need to familiarize yourself with the effects of dark psychology in the community, including families as well as different individuals.

While some people restrain this character, some will take action upon their feelings, thereby delving into certain characters.

Dark psychology also seeks to comprehend the different thoughts and feelings, as well as perceptions that may lead to existing human predatory behavior.

It assumes that the production is natural and purposive and carries some rational and goal-oriented elements at that time.

The remaining percentages under the umbrella of dark psychology refer to the brutalization of the victims without any purposeful intent, coupled with a reasonably defined science as well as religious dogma.

In the next century, there will be predators as well as their acts of different actions of theft, violence, coupled with abuse.

It'll become a major global as well as an international epidemic that will affect society. There will also be cyberbullies and sexual predators that will harm different people.

Just as portrayed in the study of dark psychology, abuse is going to become an international phenomenon that will affect every part of the earth.

As such, the theory of predators takes up the same framework. However, it revolves around the abuse as well as the assault of different people using information and communications technology.

With that said, egoism, psychopathy, sadism, as well as spitefulness are some of the traits that have been standing in for dark psychology.

Results from a project show that was spearheaded by various scientific researchers also indicated that these traits stand for the dark sides of the human personality.

They are defined as the dark core.

Therefore, if you have one or more of these traits, you are likely to possess others as well. In the world of history, life is full of perfect examples that people are using to exude their characters while acting mercilessly towards others.

Most of these individuals are not only selfish but self-centered.

They are barely supporting their friends and relatives in handling their projects. For that reason, there are different names for such traits.

Some are known as psychopaths, while others are better defined as narcissists.

While at first glance these traits appear to be well defined such that the differences can be seen, and they seem more acceptable at first glance, they also appear to be a bit confusing for learners who are seeking to understand the effects of dark psychology in the community.

As such, most dark traits have been misunderstood by people seeking to learn more about psychology and understand their friends as well as relatives.

New research on the same indicates that other traits that can be categorized in this discipline are such as sadism and spitefulness.

Many dark traits can be comprehended as a major flavored manifestation of the common underlying issue that directs researchers to disposition.

With that said, the dark core of a person's personality is what is defined as dark psychology.

It implies that if a person is known for having the tendency of exuding these dark traits; they are also likely to have a strong, viable additional trait.

According to research, the common denominator, in this case, is the D-factor which can also be defined as the general main tendency of a person's ability to maximize their utility by disregarding and accepting the disutility of other individuals.

This is usually accompanied by the belief that serves as a justification. In other words, it implies that dark traits can easily be traced back to the tendency of putting one's own objective as well as interests over other people's preferences.

This act is usually to the extent of rejoicing when another person encounters any misfortune in life.

The main intention is to hurt others while pleasing one.

The research-based on this study indicated that dark traits come along with certain justifications that can generally be understood as different instances of the common core.

While these aspects may be different in different ways, they all sum up to one major trait that is known as dark psychology.

The justifications point to narcissism since there's an aspect of provocative characters. A psychology professor known as Ingo

Zettler has demonstrated how the common denominator applies in the study of dark psychology.

Here are a few factors he pointed out towards egoism, moral disengagement, self-interest, spitefulness, psychopathy, Machiavellianism, and psychological entitlement. These are some of the important elements he realized that needed the input of trained professionals in deciphering the truth behind their effects on humanity.

In a different series of over 2,000 individuals, moderators realized that most people who were asked to what extent they agreed to disagree with sentiments such as it's challenging to delve into projects without being manipulative here and there, and, it's worth the struggle of trying to find out what the project really entails exuded tendencies of aggression as well as impulsivity.

These are the main measures of selfishness, as well as unethical characters and behavior.

The researchers also mapped out the main D–factor, which ended up being published in the academic journal of psychological reviews.

The subject can largely be compared to the works of Charles Spearman, which were published more than 100 years ago when he stated that people who often score highly in a certain type of intelligence test would most likely score highly in a different test. This is because there is a general aspect of both cases.

In that same way, it was established that the dark elements of the human brain and personality have a certain common denominator which implies that one can easily say that they are in the expression of the dispositional tendency.

For instance, in a person, the dark factor is usually manifested as narcissism and psychopathy.

It may also be any other form of a dark trait such as a combination of the two. However, with the correct mapping of the common denominator, one may easily ascertain that a person has the dark factor in their brain.

This is because the element indicates how likely an individual is to engage in different behaviors linked to one or more of the dark traits.

An individual who exudes some of these traits is likely to carry some elements of malevolent behavior, too.

They are likely to humiliate other people by cheating, lying, as well as stealing. The updated nine dark traits aren't the same.

They may also result in various kinds of characters. Nonetheless, at the core of these traits, every trait can majorly result in certain kinds of behaviors that end up setting them apart from the rest.

The dark traits in a person are not the same for everyone.

Every element in those traits differs in different persons.

At the core of the characters, the dark traits have common elements that may end up setting them apart.

Knowledge regarding this dark core can also play an important role in the life of researchers as well as therapists who often work with specified people in assessing the existing dark personalities in individuals.

As it may be, the dark trait and factor that affects various types of reckless as well as malicious person's behaviors in addition to actions have often been reported on media. For instance, it has been seen in extreme cases, that many of these cases involve people who lie and manipulate others, thereby ending up killing them.

It has also been established that some of these people with the D-factor of characters have ended up deceiving officials in the public sector.

Here, vast and extensive knowledge regarding a person's D-factor can be a useful tool in assessing a person's traits in the long run.

Also, it's going to be used against them to prevent them from taking more actions against humanity.

A Major Fact Box of Dark Psychology

Dark psychology is a powerful force that works in the real world today. It's one of those factors that majorly control the world in many ways.

It's used by the world's most powerful influencers to control most of the actions taking place in different scenes, including politics, the health sector, and the entire economy generally. It is also one of the main forces behind different industries across the world.

Dark psychology has been applied by professionals who are aware of its implications in the world and its economy.

You should not be at risk of receiving the actions of those people who understand this game better.

As such, many people are encouraged to find the real meaning of this subject before associating with other people in different matters.

It seeks to identify the traits involved in dark psychology while addressing some of the impending issues that need to be dealt with.

In the long run, these also address some of the main applications of dark psychology not only as a subject but a trait in many people who would like to manipulate others.

In the subject of dark psychology, ideas are usually illuminated using various examples to make the duty of comprehending the actual factors slightly easier.

As a learner, you're likely to come across different studies that analyze the application of dark psychology in matters of real life.

You will also have a clear understanding of the issues affecting the center of humanity, especially when it comes to seeking the truth about how people treat each other.

People with dark market traits are often considered to be callous, cold, dishonest, as well as impulsive in every action they take.

At their workplaces, these individuals can easily endanger the eventual success of their teams while seeking to become the best versions of themselves to be identified as winners in the long run. Also, one other popular conception is that they may risk the lives of their team members without their knowledge.

Chapter 8.
When the Opponent Is a Manipulator

If the negotiating partner is a genius of communication, then it is best to find a way to make him or her replaced with a less talented one. Of course, this is possible in the sense that this person is not the decision-maker.

You can discredit. You can look for the possibility of transferring such a fellow to another project—preferably in another city. You can find him other life concerns.

Another good way is to find someone who can influence him. Now, I will write in more detail.

Golden Key

Someone is influencing each of us. Sometimes, someone's opinion is important; sometimes, the attitude; sometimes, the wishes—head, wife, lover, friend, a famous magazine, public opinion in the person of "Aunt Tasha," the cleaning lady.

If you can figure out people whose opinion is important for your future interlocutor, consider that you have already practically prepared the ground for negotiations—unless, of course, you can influence them.

And when they tell him about ten times from different sources how wonderful you are, how good it is to deal with you, how important it is to listen to your opinion and go towards you, you just have to appear and voice your proposal.

Become a Mythical Person

Experienced negotiators collect all available information about the other side. So make sure that all available information about you plays on you. Rumors, gossip, stories, legends—create a myth about you! And make it available to the masses. Plus, the reputation, of course, has not been canceled.

Let your opponents get conflicting, sometimes erroneous, mysterious information about you. Or they just gain the belief that you need to be friends, you need to be taken care of, cared for, and cherished.

Arouse Emotions

If you control emotions in a conversation, you control enough. You may have gaps in the argument and stretch in the logic. You may not have any normal rationale at all. If only it depended on you what the interlocutor will experience.

The ability to arouse interest, delight, joy, pleasure, curiosity, attraction, fear, doubt, insecurity, anger, disgust—this is all that is necessary for success in negotiations. If it is, the rest will follow.

If the interlocutor does not see the logic in your words, but he likes your ideas, he will come up with the logic himself. If the opponent does not agree with your arguments, but at the same time feels sadness and regret, he will be able to convince himself. Control your emotions, and you will succeed.

The State of the Interlocutor

It became clear that the creators were sitting here in the morning—in their eyes smoldered the light of the indescribable stupidity that the brain always emanates, exhausted by hours of brainstorming. —Anonymous.

It can also be influenced. Directly and indirectly. If you think of negotiations for your interlocutor's deadline, and he just doesn't physically have time to look for other options, his condition is good for you. Especially if you manage to pull the time politely. If this morning he was "accidentally" poured with mud over his car, he will not be very comfortable. If during a meeting with you they called him and told him the good news, he will be more generous. If he holds a cup of roasting coffee poured to the top, part of his attention will be riveted to her.

Biorhythms, state of health, "random" meetings, background music, lack of sleep, day of the week—all this and much more affects the physical and psychological state of the interlocutor. And if you competently think about how to use all this, you can "make" even the best negotiator.

Pain Points, Weaknesses, Fears, Doubts

"Sir," a student asked, thinking, "How did you find out that she loves nuggets so much?"

"Learn to use the Internet, Daria," I explained. A fool in the "interests" is everywhere written in plain text.

Any friends of his, old and new, information about the psychotype, observation of behavior and reactions—any strength has a dual weakness, so even laudatory reviews will tell you a lot. Just collect the information. We analyze. We are looking for optimal methods of exposure—because it would be wrong to use this information head-on. Only leave as a last resort.

Play on Weaknesses

Regrettably, the vast majority of people are cars. In the sense that they live quite mechanically. There is a stimulus—there will be a reaction. Press the button—you get the result. Already on this alone, you can build a huge number of effective manipulations.

Now, it is important for us that when you click on some buttons, people completely automatically give out stormy experiences. It is necessary to shout at someone, threaten another, praise the third, admire the fourth, show the fifth to the sixth, show the "sex-friendly" object, take the seventh away—of course, different things affect different people. Therefore, if the interlocutor did not give a significant reaction to one provocation, you need to move on to another.

To do this, you need to know the list of basic human weaknesses. For example, I offer these:

- Superiority
- Greed
- Pity
- Sex
- Patriotism
- Masculinity
- Femininity
- Fear
- Wine
- Generosity
- Envy
- Jealousy
- Justice
- "Weak?"

Over time, you will learn to determine by eye what this or that person will do. In the meantime, you can just do a bust. Or even switch to another way to set your interlocutor off balance for your antics to work.

We Are Not Robots; Robots Are Not We

Information collection is standard. We are looking for patterns in the spirit of, "In the situation 'X,' he acts 'U.'" Accordingly, we can provoke the "U" we need by creating the corresponding "X." For example, when they praise his car, he blurs with a happy smile. Clearly, what needs to be done to make him smile? If he agrees only to the third proposal, the first two cannot be soared. And the third is to make it profitable for us.

On the other hand, if we know what external signs are responsible for what internal reaction, we actually "read the thoughts" of the interlocutor—which is convenient. Look for patterns!

Territory Development

They say that Special Forces differ from ordinary well-physically and psychologically trained troops in only one: the completeness and quality of information about the enemy and the place of the future massacre. Under this information, a model of the future theater of operations is built. Then tactical combat schemes are planned and practiced to be automatic. Therefore, special forces and can destroy many times superior enemy, and even on its territory.

If the information is false, the Special Forces are doomed. And no hand-to-hand combat with mark shooting helps them—foreign territory.

The funny thing is that many people go to important "meetings" with them, not even having mastered their own territory. What really does fit into any framework, you should still propose to master it.

The Best Alternative to Negotiations

If negotiations fail, what will happen to you? Where are you going to go? Who to contact? A simple fact: if the alternatives you have are the sea, you are calm, like a boa constrictor, easily take risks, and can play on the verge of a foul. And the attitude arises—that same game. If you have a rich choice, you will not put up with the inconvenience. If there is no choice, you will have to come to terms. If you have nothing to fear, you will not use harsh and ugly methods. People pressed against the wall are capable of any meanness.

Look for alternatives! Expand your selection! Explore the market. Offer to many. And when the price of defeat falls, there will be significantly more victories.

Let the Walls Help You

"Maybe I should not go to the palace?"

- How to walk! Sorrel raised his voice. "I will need a henchman."

- A henchman?

- Well, yes. One who listens to me—errs, cast spells—and admires them: the very first degree of apprenticeship.

It is good when it depends on us where we will meet with the interlocutor! After all, we can make everything play for us. Or a lot. The ideal situation is when the territory is fully developed by you but is not familiar to him at all. Then you have almost won.

If everyone around you shows honor, the interlocutor inevitably imbues with respect. If the music helps to create the right mood sounds, it's also good. If it depends on you what will be served on the table, you have an advantage. If everything that happens does involuntarily distract his attention, and you are used to it, everything is just wonderful.

The appearance and disappearance of certain people. Calls to mobile, Shine, Music, and Furniture. Create an atmosphere! And do not forget about your own convenience. Let your acquaintance psychologist sit next door—he will tell you how to behave and point out mistakes. Let convenient access to the Internet be nearby if you need quick reference information. Let your friend be here, next to whom you will be "knee-deep in the sea of affairs." The territory is a creative affair.

Who Is Around?

If your support group is around, with an approving hum that meets all your remarks and is ready to boo any creep in your direction, the opponent will be hard.

Anyway, no matter who is nearby, it is sometimes more useful to influence the interlocutor through the audience. Very often, speakers do not turn to the opponent, who will object anyway, but to the public, which will support it sooner. Let your words and actions look beautiful. Attractive. And well, if he himself will be shy of his actions. Witnesses determine!

Therefore, by the way, it can be useful to invite rude negotiators with their wives—for a dinner party, for example. And then, they automatically lose all the advantages of the usual style of communication—against the background of a man who, in theory, should have played on his side.

Leeway

Everything is clear here: we create the maximum margin of time for ourselves and adjust to the minimum margin for the other side. Then we are calm, and time plays on us. And the opponent twitches. Because time is playing against him.

Where Is the World Heading?

Where are oil prices moving? What is the situation with the labor market? Where does the political course go? What major competitors will enter the market soon? And if you know what market is, political, cultural, etc. situations will play on you at some point, you can guess.

Chapter 9.
Setting Boundary Not to Be Manipulated

By now, you must have the ability to know the value of setting limits for both personal and relationship growth. Many people will have a hard time establishing and maintain boundaries because of some misconceptions. Because they are scared of the repercussions, such borders can have on their values and their lifestyle.

For instance, some individuals hesitate about losing all their friends when their limits appear to be too high and unrealistic. It is essential to handle common boundary myths and accept reality to set limits effectively.

Misconception #1: I May Look Self-Centered If I Set Boundaries

This misconception or objection is frequently raised by people who believe or feared being considered as self-centered or self-indulgent when they set boundaries. Many people are scared of being accused of doing not have issues for others when they set borders. Hence they offer upsetting such limits. In reality, setting boundaries does not make you self-centered; setting limits will help you take care of others, while you safeguard yourself from being at the receiving end of every misgiving. Individuals who set boundaries the most are typically the most caring ones in the world because they have discovered that through borders, their requirements have been taken care of; for this reason, they have lots of energy and time to take care of the needs of others.

All our needs, desires, and selfishness only consider our desires, whereas borders think about our needs. When we concentrate on our desires, we might lose focus and balance, and somewhat of pursuing our healthy goals through setting limits, selfishness might force us to work to please others. Trying to satisfy our needs does not make such requirements bad.

Misconception #2: Boundaries Are Symptoms of Disobedience and Un-Submissiveness

Many people are scared that setting boundaries or limits will signal to their partners, co-workers, friends, or bosses that they are disobedient and rebellious. Some people think that saying "No" to something good just implies they are unresponsive. Thus they take part in every social event or take whatever that is thrown at them. Doing everything that comes, your doing has no spiritual or psychological worth. When you do things out of your inner voice, however, your heart is not in it, and then you are wasting your time and trying to please others. Focus on setting borders in whatever you do so that you don't do too much.

Outwardly need something when we mean No merely makes you a liar. If we state No to great things only because of our self-centered desires, then such a limit makes you disobedient.

Misconception # 3: Setting Limits Indicates I Am Always Upset

For many novices who are just setting borders, they may realize that they suddenly begin to tell the truth and take responsibility for all their actions. These people may feel that some type of "anger cloud is surrounding them," many especially when they become conscious where their limits are being violated. When you start setting boundaries, you might fear that you can be offended easily, and this might get you confused. This is simply one of the essential things you may experience at the beginning of setting a limit; however, you will overcome it when individuals start to understand what you stand for. Borders do not cause anger in us; however, if you see the limit set as the source of your passion, and then you misunderstand your emotions. Your emotions must be the signals that need to tell you about something—for instance, your fear ought to advise you to move away from a dangerous situation, while anger needs to ask you to challenge an imminent risk.

You ought to remember that a mad circumstance is a warning that you are in imminent danger of being attacked or injured. For this reason, anger ought to be viewed as a positive indication that you will be manipulated, or your boundary will be violated. While your worry might tell you to withdraw from a situation, anger will help you advance and protect your fence. There is no reason to be scared when your boundaries are being breached; instead, the violence should help you not to be violent; however, affordable way to inform the violator to stop breaking your borders.

Don't simply let your anger out; instead, you need to discover to protect whatever is yours more properly without showing unfavorable feelings.

Misconception #4: When I Begin Creating Borders, I Might Be Injured by Others

When you set limits with people who do not regard constraints, it is frequently complicated. Indeed, many people don't like it when we present our arguments and viewpoints, and may snap at us or simply withdraw from connecting with us. However, this does not mean you need to treat people gently always because they don't appreciate your border. You should not refrain from reality, because those who enjoy the truth will quickly want to associate with you. It is essential to be liked by people who understand the fact than to be disliked by many who wish to oppress and take advantage of you.

Ask yourself the question; what if the person who hates you for your borders is your spouse? Will you then abide by no boundary guidelines just to maintain peace in your relationship? Or will you just endure his wrong sides and let him breach your borders and still abandon you. If you hesitate to the survival of your relationship and keep allowing your partner to maltreat you, then you might not have the guts to set the boundaries. It is ideal to discover the hidden character of your partner and solve all fundamental problems instead of preventing the problem.

It is highly likely that you will get hurt from setting borders; however, your relationship will likely end up being deeper.

Misconception #5: When I Set Limits I Might Injure Others

You may end up frustrating other people occasionally when you set boundaries, particularly when you value the happiness of such people. Some of the cases where you might hurt people when you set a limit to consist of:

• When a friend desires to borrow your car when you need it

• People might call you for a social gathering preparation, which is when you are physically down, or

• When a relative enters into a difficult financial situation; however, you can't loan him the specific quantity because you have some monetary responsibilities to care for.

Depending on how you see boundaries, you might harm or might not injure others. However, nothing can be much better than knowing the truth, and the truth is that setting borders around your treasures is the only way you can safeguard them from being taken, ruined, or trampled with. When you set boundaries for the wrong function or motive, then you might hurt the ideal people. Still, you need to remember that saying No for the best reason will not cause injury to other people, although it might trigger discomfort, and they need to look elsewhere for the same favor.

It is not your responsibility to meet the requirements of everyone; though you must do everything possible to help others achieve their goals (however not at the hindrance of your happiness). You should help others quickly when you have the resources to do so, and even when somebody dares to have a problem. You might have other more significant issues to compete with, for this reason; you need to try to fix the most critical problems in your own life before thinking about meeting the needs of others. Sometimes you might be the one who gets declined; hence, you need to develop some supportive relationships where you do not enslave yourself because of others.

Misconception #6: Boundaries Might Become Difficult to Accept

Some people hesitate to establish boundaries because of the bad experiences they had in the past regarding previous borders that were set for them. Obtaining to accept the limits set by others can be unpleasant. Given that nobody likes to be declined, you need to prepare your mind for unfavorable answers you get when you cross the boundaries set by others. You may ask yourself, why is it difficult for people to accept bounds?

- During your youth, you may have been hurt by certain unsuitable limits set by people. When parents set borders around their kids, for example, the kids might feel some sense of not being wanted, and this may follow them through their adult years, and often feel unaccepted when the word "No" is said to them. The bright side is that old problems don't have to stick in your memory correctly when you discover to accept other people's limits.
- Individuals who were gravely injured by borders in their youth typically attempt to leave from the harmed by satisfying the same bounds against others. Setting boundaries on other people cannot allow you to impost hatred on them because they will just move away from you for the best reason. Never predict your old feelings from the boundaries set for you, for your kids, good friends, colleagues, and other people around you.
- The inability to accept limits set by others, specifically in your marital life, might tend to do with your objectives of unfaithfulness to your partner.

- If your emotional satisfaction will always depend on your spouse's being on your side at all times, then something is not right about the relationship because you are the only one who set borders.
- Failure to accept boundaries may show somebody has problems in taking responsibility. Often, many people are accustomed to counting on people to save them from problems they deliberately induced themselves. These people believe the duties of their well-being remain in the hands of others; for this reason, they feel dejected when their recipients do not satisfy such requirements. When you learn to take responsibility for your own life, you will be positive about setting limits.

Misconception #7: Boundaries May Result in Feelings of Guilt

This is another misconception many people can't comprehend, the factor being that the sense of responsibility may become an obstacle for them in setting borders that can be advantageous. It is difficult to say No to somebody who has helped us in the past, particularly with money, effort, and time. All you need to do is show thankfulness for what has been done for you, instead of setting boundaries. Many are not comfortable taking gifts because we always think sometimes we need to pay in return. And some people do not wish to accept presents any longer because they do not want to fret about repaying in the future.

Some people do not give selflessly; however, they give for future purposes. You can discriminate between these people by the way they respond after you thank them for their gesture—Kind givers don't also wait on you to thank them because they need nothing from you. If the giver is outraged by doing you a favor, then the person sees the present as a financial investment. If your appreciation is enough, then he or she probably wants absolutely nothing in return.

The concern of thankfulness and borders should be kept different because limits must not be nullified sense of appreciation; thus, this misconception holds no weight.

Conclusion

From a psychological perspective, manipulation is an art that involves not only hiding bad intentions or aggressive behavior but also the ability to identify the emotional vulnerabilities of the other, and then implement the best strategies to manage them.

How to Avoid Being Manipulated

Know your fundamental rights. To avoid or stop manipulation, you must be aware of your rights as a person:

1. Right to be treated with respect.
2. The right to express your feelings, opinions, and desires, even if they differ from those of others.
3. The right to set your priorities.
4. The right to say "no" without feeling guilty.
5. The right to protect yourself from physical, mental, and emotional threats.
6. The right to plan a happy and healthy life.

These fundamental rights represent boundaries that others should not cross, and you should not feel bad about standing up for them.

- **Say "no" firmly.** You can refuse to do anything you are not comfortable with. It is your right. Evaluate the request and, if you don't want to give in to the demand, say "no" firmly. It is better not to give too many explanations to a manipulator because he/she will assume it as a weakness or a sense of guilt, so it is likely that he/she will continue to pressure you. A "I'm sorry, but I won't do it," is usually enough.

- **Avoid the self-blame mechanism.** The emotional manipulator will try to exploit your weaknesses, so he/she will try to make you feel guilty or inadequate. Do not fall into their trap, do not allow their words or actions to generate a feeling of guilt. Ask yourself if you are being treated with genuine respect, if the demand is reasonable, and if you feel comfortable meeting it.

- **Use time to your advantage.** In many instances, the emotional manipulator pushes so that his victim doesn't have time to think. They want an immediate response and maximize the pressure to control the situation. Therefore, a good strategy is to buy time to evaluate what he is asking for. When you say, "I'll think about it," you are also letting him/her know that you are not willing to fall into their trap and that you will not let them pressure you so easily.

- **Pay more attention to actions than words.** One of the best ways to spot an emotional manipulator is to pay more attention to their actions than their words. Often these people, especially early in the relationship, are charming and even flattering, but if you look closely, you'll find that their behaviors say otherwise. That dichotomy is very helpful in uncovering emotional manipulation in a relationship because a person who claims to love you but continually pressures you and relegates your needs to the background is probably trying to manipulate you.

- **Ask questions and clarify.** Emotional manipulators often play with ambiguity and take advantage of the fact that their victims do not usually stand up to them. Therefore, when in doubt, it is best to rethink their demands. When you hear an unreasonable request, ask back to try to make the person aware of what they are doing.

- **Establish a psychological distance.** If you believe that the manipulator will not respect your rights, it is advisable to establish a polite relationship, but with certain limits that prevent him/her from accessing your privacy, so that you can protect your emotional balance.

- **Ask for psychological help (if you need it).** If you feel that you are in a toxic relationship in which another person tries to manipulate you emotionally and does not respect you but you cannot get out of it, even though you know that this relationship is hurting you, it is time to ask for help from a psychologist.

www.ingramcontent.com/pod-product-compliance
Lightning Source LLC
Chambersburg PA
CBHW062139100526
44589CB00014B/1623